A BOOK ABOUT GOD

BY FLORENCE MARY FITCH

Illustrated by LEONARD WEISGARD

LOTHROP, LEE AND SHEPARD COMPANY   NEW YORK

Copyright, 1953, by Lothrop, Lee & Shepard Co., Inc. Library of Congress Catalog Card Number 53-6735. All rights reserved. Printed in U.S.A.

13   14   15   75   74   73

Everyone wonders about God...
Sometimes on a sunny afternoon
We look up at the blue sky
Sometimes on a winter night
When the stars are big and bright
We think about Him
And wish we could see Him
But we don't need to see God
    to know what He is like
We only need to think about the
    things that are like Him

The sky is like God...
Bright by day with the light
of the sun
Restful and friendly at night
with moon and stars

The sun is like God...

    It is always shining

Flowers turn their faces

    toward the sun

Trees stretch out their branches

    to reach the sunshine

And spread their leaves till

    every one receives the light

The sun draws each growing thing

    unto itself

And gives it life and strength

Even on cloudy days
    we see the sun's light
    and feel its warmth
Even at night when we cannot
    see the sun
The moon reflects some
    of its light

The air is like God...
Air is all around us
Even though we do not see it
    we feel its warmth
    and its coolness
Without air outside us and
    within us we cannot live
Without God we cannot live

The rain is like God's love
    falling gently upon the earth
    filling rivers and streams
    and springs
We do not see the rain feeding
    the roots of plants and
    helping the seeds to sprout
But we see the grass grow
    the flowers blossom
    and the fruits ripen

We see God's life
      in every growing thing
In trees all beautiful
      with little leaves in spring
Deep and green with the cool
      dark shade of summer

Burning bright
      with colors of fall

In winter loveliest of all

The mountains and hills are
like God...
Guarding families and homes
Protecting them from storms
that sweep around them
When we look up at the hills
we think about God

And we remember the sea...

The sea that stretches on and on

far beyond our sight

The sea that on the surface

moves as it will

But deep down is quiet and still

and full of mystery

God is like the sea

All things beautiful
    are like God
God is like all these
    and more…
No one can count
    the stars in the sky
No one can count
    the ways God shows
His love